AN E
BY THE EDITORS
OF CHRISTIANITY TODAY

HOW TO
PICK A
PRESIDENT

CLINTON, TRUMP, OR ?

WITH CONTRIBUTIONS BY
ANDY CROUCH
ED STETZER
LEITH ANDERSON
MARK GALLI
RUSSELL MOORE
CARLOS CAMPO
AND OTHERS

From Christianity Today

Copyright © 2016 Christianity Today

Published by Christianity Today,
465 Gundersen Dr., Carol Stream, Illinois 60188

ChristianityToday.com

How to Pick a President
Ver. 2.0

How to Pick a President

TABLE OF CONTENTS

LET US REASON TOGETHER

n election is a moral horror, as bad as a battle except for the blood; a mud bath for every soul concerned in it." So said the famous playwright and essayist George Bernard Shaw. Considering some elections in American history—many would point to this current election season in particular—Shaw's comment is hardly hyperbole.

It's one reason we often find ourselves hating politics. Progress on crucial moral issues is painstakingly hard to achieve. We often feel like we're taking one step forward and two steps back, in fact—and that's when everyone is behaving properly! But in times like these, when invective and slander are a regular feature of political life, we want to throw up our arms in despair.

Christians have sometimes taken that route, championing a theology that justifies political indifference. But most Christians beg to differ. As burdensome as political life can sometimes be, we know we are called not merely to honor and pray for our leaders. Especially in a democracy, we're also called to elect and to serve as leaders. And most years we're happy to do so, because we know that political battles are often over issues of great moral import. In fact, in every election, substantive moral issues are at stake.

We hope that this CT Book will help you think more deeply and wisely about your political responsibilities this election season—whether that means running for office, working for a candidate, or simply casting a vote.

To that end we've gathered what we think have been the most thoughtful *Christianity Today* articles on politics. Some are classics that remain even more relevant than the year of their original publication. Others have been crafted during this political season. They do not all agree with one another—and that's as it should be. Evangelicals are not a political monolith. We're not trying to tell you how to vote, but to help you think about your vote this season.

The first section looks at the qualities Christians look for in a national leader.

We begin with a CT classic: "How to Pick a President," by Mark McCloskey and Daniel Taylor. McCloskey is professor of transformational leadership at Bethel Seminary, in St. Paul, Minnesota. His most recent book is *The Art of Virtue-Based Transformational Leadership*. Taylor received his Ph.D. from Emory University and is the author of many books, including his most recent novel, *Death Comes to the Deconstructionist*, which won the 2016 book award in fiction from *Christianity Today*. Together they penned a very wise essay on criteria Christians should use in casting their presidential vote.

Next, Andy Crouch, executive editor of *Christianity Today,* zeroes in on one neglected quality that great leaders need. It is based on his latest book, *Strong and Weak: Embracing a Life of Love, Risk and True Flourishing* (InterVarsity Press)—whose thesis he brings to bear in this short essay.

Many voters wonder about a President's personal faith. But does a

President's faith make a difference in how a President governs? Do faith and virtue actually matter once a person is in the White House? Gary Scott Smith of Grove City College, author of *Religion in the Oval Office: The Religious Lives of American Presidents,* tries to answer these questions in an interview with CT editors.

Part two looks at a few aspects of this particular election.

In every election season, and in this one in particular, pollsters claim to know how evangelicals have or will vote. But what do they mean by *evangelical?* And does it correspond to evangelicalism in churches across America? Not usually, conclude Leith Anderson and Ed Stetzer. Anderson is president of the National Association of Evangelicals in Washington, D.C., and Stetzer is executive director of the Billy Graham Center for Evangelism in Wheaton, Illinois. They've come up with a new way to define evangelicals, which suggests most pollsters have misunderstood who they are and what they stand for politically.

Mark Galli, editor of *Christianity Today,* weighs in on a perennial temptation, especially in this election year: Can we narrow our voting choices down to one issue in good conscience?

Russell Moore wonders, if we believe that both candidates are hopelessly compromised, should we vote for the lesser of two evils? His has been a minority view this election season, but we felt it important to include in this book. Moore is president of the Ethics and Religious Liberty Commission of the Southern Baptist Convention and author of *Onward: Engaging the Culture Without Losing the Gospel.*

Hispanics have been at the forefront this election season, with Donald Trump's many promises to build a wall on our southern border, not to mention his disparaging remarks about Hispanics. But it hasn't automatically pushed Hispanics toward Hillary Clinton. Carlos Campo, president of Ashland University and leader of the educational arm of the National Hispanic Leadership Conference,

explains the voting quandary Hispanic evangelicals find themselves in.

This particular election has made many a Christian despair about our
electoral process. Chris Horst sees a silver lining in what many are calling the most discouraging election in their memory. Horst is the vice
president of development at HOPE International, author of *Mission
Drift*, and founder of dadcraft.

The book's third section contains two articles designed to give us hope
in any election season, and especially in this one.

Dietrich Bonhoeffer knew a thing or two about living in troubling
political times. Ryan Hoselton, a doctoral student in church history
at Universität Heidelberg in Germany, unpacks one of Bonhoeffer's
sermons that was preached when fear gripped German Christians as
Hitler rose to power. Though our situation is not as bad as 1930s Germany, fear saturates our current political conversation. This essay is
a nice antidote.

Finally, we offer a classic by the late Charles Colson, who worked with
Anne Morse on this final essay. It's a reminder that politics can be,
despite its immense challenges, a joy-filled opportunity for those who
see it through the eyes of faith. Anne Morse is a senior writer with the
Wilberforce Forum and the Charles Colson Prison Fellowship Ministries; she is also a frequent contributor to *National Review Online*.
Colson was founder of Prison Fellowship and the Colson Center, and
served as special counsel to President Richard Nixon. He personally
knew the curses and blessings of politics, and his encouragement to
stay engaged carries not a little weight.

We've included an appendix that outlines what the National Association of Evangelicals believes are issues that should be priorities for
Christians. It is an excerpt from the NAE's document, "For the Health
of the Nation," and it outlines seven voting issues: religious freedom,
family life, sanctity of life, care for the poor, human rights, peacemaking, and creation care. While readers will certainly add or subtract from

this list, it seems like a good starting point for a discussion on priorities for the current election.

To that end, we trust much discussion will result from reading this little volume. It can be used profitably in small groups, Sunday school classes, and other settings where Christians want to sit down and reason together (Is. 1:18) about their political life.

—*The Editors of* Christianity Today

PART ONE

QUALITIES OF A NATIONAL LEADER

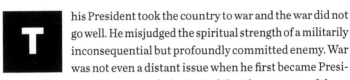

CHAPTER 1

VIRTUE VERSUS POLICY

BY MARK McCLOSKEY & DANIEL TAYLOR

his President took the country to war and the war did not go well. He misjudged the spiritual strength of a militarily inconsequential but profoundly committed enemy. War was not even a distant issue when he first became President, and he became increasingly frustrated that the unsuccessful war defined his presidency. Testy exchanges with journalists caused him to almost abandon news conferences, he was openly mocked on television and on the street, and his popularity ratings plummeted. Never one to seek wide counsel, he increasingly surrounded himself only with advisers who gave him good news, who told him what he wanted to hear.

No, his name is not George Bush. His name was Lyndon Johnson.

"I am not going to lose Vietnam," Johnson said. "*I* am not going to be the President who saw Southeast Asia go the way China went." It is significant that Johnson thought of the war in the first person—"I am not going to lose." Johnson had a famously monumental ego and soaring ambition. Friends, fellow politicians, and historians consistently

13

report that what motivated Johnson from his schoolboy days to his presidency was a pure lust for power and control unusual even for a politician. As Johnson's biographer Robert Caro observes, "Johnson's ambition was uncommon—in the degree to which it was unencumbered by even the slightest excess weight of ideology, of philosophy, of principles, of beliefs."

Lyndon Johnson edited reality to suit his needs. Anyone who disagreed with him on Vietnam policy was a "knee-jerk liberal," "crackpot," "nervous Nellie," or "troublemaker." There was no such thing for him as loyal dissent. Lyndon Johnson was as politically competent as any President in history (and he used that competence for good in getting passed the 1964 Civil Rights Act). He lacked, however, the wisdom and moral courage necessary to keep this country from far deeper entanglement in a disastrous war.

Iraq is not Vietnam. George Bush is not Lyndon Johnson. Taking the country to war is not automatically wrong. But grave decisions of war and peace, life and death, prosperity and privation—on the domestic and international fronts—are made by Presidents during their time in office. At election time, we the people decide who our decision makers will be. And we too often decide poorly, because we ask the wrong questions.

We make the same mistake as one grumpy CNN commentator, who said during the 2008 election: "What we need from these candidates are details of how they are going to solve our problems. How are they going to stop the slide of the dollar? How are they going to get the troops home from Iraq? How are they going to fix Social Security? That's what we need to know." Grumpy and wrong. There's value in hearing a candidate's plans and proposals, but it's of secondary or even lesser importance. Few if any of those plans and proposals will survive the political process intact. When it comes to picking a President, Gandhi had it right: "The obligation of accepting a position of power is to be, above all else, a good human being."

"You've got to be kidding," one hears our CNN commentator saying. "'Good human being'? Who's to say what constitutes a 'good human being'? I want someone competent to run the country." Wrong again. Competence without virtue is poisonous. It simply makes one more effective at doing wrong. Furthermore, being virtuous is, in itself, an expression of competence. Since virtue is a requirement for leadership, a lack of virtue in a leader is a sign of incompetence and grounds enough for rejecting that leadership. Virtue is a personal matter, but it is never wholly a private one, certainly not in a President.

A SUITE OF VALUES-SOAKED ABILITIES

The ancient Greeks created most of our vocabulary of virtue and saw virtue as central to politics. In fact, it was wrestling with the question of the kind of leader a community required that led them to investigate virtue, and that made virtue a practical, not merely a philosophical, consideration.

Virtue—moral and physical—was to the Greeks a force, a capacity to do something, a personal power that enabled one to influence and shape oneself and one's community for the better. Virtue was practical, specific, and verifiable. The Greeks saw virtue as intimately connected with character, which can be defined as the working out of values in actual life—values lived—the intersection in the everyday world of stated values with choices and actions. For the Greeks it was meaningless to talk about values (think "family values" or "justice for the poor") apart from concrete actions that render those values visible and useful. And such actions were only virtues if they were recurring, becoming so ingrained in a person's responses to life that they were moral habits, reflexes, something that flowed almost automatically from one's essential nature. Virtue was not a given of birth or instinct, but must be learned and reinforced (hence, education centered on training in virtue).

Virtue is a suite of values-soaked abilities that in active combination form a person's character and give shape to a life. Our choices and actions both reveal and reinforce our character. You cannot judge whether a person will be a good leader—a good President—without knowing and evaluating his or her character—how life has stamped or marked them. A President is, among other things, a decision maker. Decisions flow out of values and experience, that is, out of character.

The classical virtues, embraced by Greeks and Romans alike, are prudence (practical wisdom), justice (fairness), fortitude (courage), and temperance (moderation). They not only thought these desirable and useful, but also believed you could not be fully human without them. Each of the four virtues makes the others possible, and a lack of any one of them renders the others ineffective. Courage without wisdom is mere foolhardiness. Justice not backed up by courage is mere wishing. And any of the other virtues is vitiated if one lacks the self-control found in moderation. Virtue involves the whole person—intellect, emotion, will, values, actions.

The other great source of virtues was Judeo-Christian, especially the virtues of faith, hope, and love. The medieval period inherited both traditions, kept virtue at the center of education, and embraced these seven as "the cardinal virtues."

So how does any of this help in choosing a President?

FROM COURAGE TO TEMPERANCE

Let's start with the virtue perhaps most universally acknowledged and admired: courage. In premodern times, the courage of a leader often had to be physical. In the last 500 years, it is more often moral. Moral courage is the ability to do what's right even when it is deeply unpopular, even dangerous. Courage is only found where there is the genuine possibility of loss—loss of friends, reputation, status, power, possessions, or, at the extremes, freedom or life.

It does not require courage to do what is popular or safe. Political leaders in a democracy must, by definition, be popular at election time or they will no longer be leaders. So it is even more difficult for a President, whose choices are not masked by being one vote among many, to be morally courageous than it is for other politicians. Ironically, to be morally courageous, a politician must be willing to forfeit the very position that gives him or her the power to make the morally courageous decision in the first place. Fail to be courageous and your country will suffer and history will criticize you; make the unpopular but morally courageous decision and we may well remove you from office.

Most would credit Lincoln with moral courage in his handling of the Civil War. More contentious cases could be made for Franklin Roosevelt's response to the Depression, for Reagan in his refusal to accept the inevitability of half the world living under Communism, and for Carter in his principled campaign for human rights in a political environment that normally only pays lip service to such things. Whoever your personal political heroes, it is likely that you admire them in significant part because they risked doing the right thing instead of the safe thing. Historian Barbara Tuchman observes, "Aware of the controlling power of ambition, corruption, and emotion, it may be that in the search for wiser government we should look for the test of character first. And the test should be moral courage."

It is not difficult to see how prudence is valuable for any leader. In both Greek and Jewish traditions, prudence or wisdom is knowledge about how to live well and the ability to put that knowledge into practice. It involves right priorities and right choices. Intelligent people can be fools. Knowledgeable people can be impractical.

It is entirely appropriate to evaluate whether a person seeking public office has lived wisely in his or her private life. Too often we attribute the wisdom to lead to someone who has merely been resourceful enough to succeed in business or some other area. We have de-stigmatized many private failures in recent years (divorce, past drug use, sexual irresponsibility), but it is still relevant to expect that public leaders show wisdom in the choices they make in their private lives.

Practical wisdom, as opposed to intelligence or knowledge, is necessary

17

to respond helpfully to the many political problems that involve competing goods or "no good choices." The illegal immigration problem sets the reasonable need to control one's borders against the pragmatic fact of what to do about the millions of illegal immigrants already here. The response to terror in the world requires a balance between the goal (security, certainly, and perhaps the extension of democracy) and the means to reach that goal (wiretapping? torture?). The political system perhaps never "solves" these issues to everyone's satisfaction, but a leader needs the virtue of practical wisdom to move us forward.

No quality is more often invoked in contemporary political campaigns than justice—frequently under the umbrella of fairness. In fact, we have trained citizens to present many of their demands in terms of what is fair and of injuries to fairness. The poor, the middle class, and the rich all contend that the tax system is not fair to them. Those who identify as LGBTQ as well as women and people of color each present themselves as victims of a society and political system that should, in the name of justice, offer them protection and redress. But so do corporations, lawyers, religious organizations, and many other social entities that by many measures are doing quite well. It is self-evident that a President must care about justice, but what does that mean and what would it look like? We should assess the nature and intensity of each candidate's commitment to justice and ask them to articulate both the foundations for their commitments and to give evidence that they have acted to make the world a fairer place. If that action was evident in their private lives even before they sought public office, so much the better. It means more than campaign platitudes and position papers about social justice and helping the poor.

Temperance, or moderation, might seem like both the least attractive of the classical virtues and the least significant for a political leader. The elder George Bush often used the vocabulary of moderation and caution and got himself satirized on television and in the comic strips as timorous and weak ("wouldn't be prudent" was a laugh line for people whose main association with the word temperance is the benighted attempt in the past century to ban alcohol). But temperance is as crucial as any of the other virtues because its lack renders them less effective.

Temperance is self-restraint, the ability to control (even say "no" to) harmful drives, impulses, and passions (one reason Aquinas thought it the most difficult virtue, even if the least lofty). It is an expression of discipline and self-mastery that allows a leader to function under pressure, including external pressure from extremists and ideologues to act rashly to accomplish immediate and simplistic goals.

Lincoln's conciliatory attitude toward the defeated South is a marked example of temperance amidst extremists (think also of Nelson Mandela). Harry Truman was noted for temperate intemperance, writing many angry letters and memos (including one calling for the destruction of every major Russian city) but having the temperance to never send them.

Personal intemperance makes a politician more susceptible to debilitating weaknesses such as anger, lust, and an inordinate need for popularity. Many argue that Bill Clinton's sexual appetites were irrelevant to his political leadership, but his famous overnight polling and use of focus groups to detect which way the popular winds were blowing suggest both an intemperate need to be liked and a lack of moral courage to make unpopular decisions. How much longer did Vietnam go on because of Lyndon Johnson's vanity and penchant for ignoring unpleasant realities, or how much greater did Nixon's bitter, personal anger grow toward peace activists? Moderation matters.

FAITH, HOPE, LOVE—IN A PRESIDENT?

Even those who acknowledge the relevance of the four classical virtues in evaluating presidential candidates might question the significance of the three biblical ones. And perhaps as virtues tied to a specific religious tradition they are potentially controversial. But to the extent that these too are universal qualities (as many social scientists and philosophers argue), they can be expressed in ways that both the religious and secular can affirm.

The ultimate expression of faith may be religious, but in nonsectarian terms it has to do with commitment to a larger story than one's individual life. Politically, faith is commitment to the story of America—its fundamental worth, its potential for good, its ability to heal its wounds. In this sense, both Martin Luther King—a prophetic critic—and Ronald Reagan—a vocal advocate—demonstrated great faith in America. The key issue in assessing this quality in a candidate is not whether they engage in happy talk about the country, but whether they are capable of calling people to have faith in its essential worth and to work to better realize that inherent possibility.

Similarly with hope. Hope is not mere wishing. It is a reasonable expectation based on past experience. It is not reasonable for me to hope to win the lottery, because I have no experiential or mathematical reason to think it will happen. It is reasonable to hope that America will be more just tomorrow than it is today because we know from history and experience that America is capable of acting justly, even if it has never succeeded in being completely just. We know that people have worked and sacrificed for justice with significant success, and so we can rightly hope to go even further (or to recover lost ground) in that direction.

This ability to inspire hopefulness, of course, must be influenced by practical wisdom, and not be mere blinkered cheerleading. Hope is an expectation of future good that is mingled with the understanding that good is never guaranteed and that the obstacles are many. Ronald Reagan's famous slogan, "It's morning in America," expressed perhaps his greatest virtue—the ability to engender hope. Again, Martin Luther King ("we shall overcome") was doing the same thing. Both had to back up those words with actions in order to make such hope a reality.

Love has its ultimate expression in the things of God and the Spirit, but it is relevant to our political and social lives as well. If love is the greatest of the biblical virtues, it is possibly also the ultimate home for all the virtues. We are courageous in order to protect people and things we love. We fight for justice for those we love (even at a distance). We exercise the self-control of moderation and seek to bring wisdom into the world for the sake of what and whom we love. Our earnest love for a certain kind of world gives us faith and hope that such a world can be brought into being.

It is very difficult to assess the quality of love in political candidates. Perhaps one manifestation of it is passion. Passion comes from the Greek word for pain or suffering. To say we love or are passionate about something is a declaration that we are willing to suffer for it. What are candidates passionate about? That is, what are they willing to suffer for? What have they spent their lives doing apart from jobs and political office? What loves or passions made them pursue political office?

VIRTUE OVER POLICIES AND IDEOLOGY

It would of course be a false dichotomy to suggest that one must choose between assessing virtue and assessing policy or ideology. Virtue and character can and should express themselves in both policy and ideology. One's virtue as a leader is inescapably revealed by ideological stances and policy decisions on, for instance, partial-birth abortion or the need for health care for all citizens. If so, why not let policy be the objective index to personal qualities and focus on such concrete things, rather than get into the messy subjectivity of virtue and character?

Chief among the many reasons is that many crucial political decisions of the future will revolve around unpredictable events and issues. In 2000, no candidate's "policy" on terrorism foresaw or was adequate for 9/11. In 2004, no candidate had a policy or ideology that would have made Hurricane Katrina greatly less painful (would even the most compassionate and competent President in 2004 have chosen, from all other needs, to spend many millions of dollars to reinforce the dikes in New Orleans?). No one in the 1970s was prepared for AIDS in the 1980s and '90s. Few people clearly foresaw the collapse of Communism, or the rise thereafter of Islamic fundamentalism. A political leader must be able to respond to ever-changing and unprecedented situations. We should vote for a person whom we believe has the qualities—the virtues, the character—to decide wisely in situations where policies, positions, and ideologies will be of little help.

In addition, campaign policies are illustrative at best and deceitful at

21

worst. Politicians offer proposals that they very well know can never be enacted in the form proposed or have the effects they claim.

And if policies are not much of a guide, neither is ideology. Even foundational political philosophies work better in textbooks and tracts than in Washington. Are we to believe, yet again, that Democratic candidates can find the money in a real Congress for all the social equity promises they make every four years? Or that Tea Party Republicans can actually, even if they want to, dramatically shrink the size of government? Or that anyone is genuinely revolutionary or powerful enough to invoke overwhelming "change" in Washington? There's a systemic momentum to government and its bureaucracies that eats ideology for lunch. Simple realism indicates we have a better chance of making a generally accurate assessment of a candidate's character—and hoping in that—than we have of using policy or ideology to predict their future actions or success.

The closer we are in time to a President or presidential campaign, the more likely we are to focus on minutiae of policy, platform, likeability, and style. But Hugh Sidey, longtime observer of Presidents, believed other things are more important: "The presidency to this day rests more on the character of the person who inhabits the office than on anything else. The founding fathers designed it that way. It was their idea to find a man in America with a great character and let him invest a tradition and shape a national character." They found that man in George Washington, a President who refused to be king and who had the virtue to walk away from power when people were begging him to hold on to it.

The greatest fear we have regarding leaders is that they will misuse the power we grant them. The corrupting potential of power is well documented. But power need not corrupt and in a virtuous person it will not. Psychologist Erich Fromm distinguishes between power used for domination and selfish ends, and what he calls "potency" or "generative power." Such power is strength for others (a definition of virtue), and it motivates creativity and service. All the proper policies and ideology and technical competency in the world will not protect a leader from

22

using power corruptly. In fact, the greatest temptation for a well-meaning leader is to use power corruptly in order to accomplish seemingly benevolent ends. The best insurance against corrupt power is to choose leaders with the combination of virtues necessary to use power well.

LOOK AT ORDINARY LIFE

How, specifically, could one ever hope to discern these things in a candidate? There is no easy or foolproof way. But start with what they do when no one is looking. Pascal observed, "The strength of a man's virtue must not be measured by his efforts, but by his ordinary life."

There is nothing ordinary about being a President. Politicians are public performers, playing always to the watchful electorate. So look at what they did and how they conducted their lives before they went on the political stage. And look at what they do when they hope no one is looking after they take office.

Look also for any record of willingness to speak and act from conviction when doing so has threatened their careers or self-interest. (It was said of George Marshall of Marshall Plan fame that "he told the truth even when it hurt his cause.") That is, where have they shown moral courage? One should not evaluate these things only in terms of whether you agree with their positions or not, but also in terms of whether they are capable of doing what is broadly unpopular (not just unpopular with their political opponents) if they believe it is right.

Explore also how they treat their opponents. Are critics seen as people to dialogue with, work with, and perhaps even learn from, or as enemies to be destroyed? How inclined are they to vilify, demonize, and use dirty tricks? How often are they intellectually dishonest or jingoistic (for instance, any claim that automatically links opposition to a war to lack of patriotism)? Johnson and Nixon are the negative poster boys here, with both Reagan and Carter getting high marks for largely refusing to engage in slash-and-burn politics.

Consider also how they respond to getting or losing power. Lincoln pointed out, "Nearly all men can stand adversity, but if you want to test a man's character, give him power." Or take it away. Virtuous leaders hold on to power loosely. They share it easily. They encourage it in others. They see it as invested in healthy institutions, not in themselves personally. Unvirtuous, and therefore dangerous, leaders accumulate power for themselves (and their causes), use it to intimidate and manipulate, to reward and punish, and never release it voluntarily. Lyndon Johnson's abusive use of power as a senator—in which he made loyalty to himself more important than either morality or ideology—hurt the nation.

Yet another place to look is how candidates have dealt with adversity in their own lives. Franklin Roosevelt, for example, overcame the effects of polio. But of course all candidates have failures in their lives, too. If a candidate is given to private anger and pettiness, or has a history of broken personal relationships, does that tell us absolutely nothing about what kind of leader he or she might be? Is that none of our business, as some would say, or very much our business if that candidate is asking to be President?

The issue is not that candidates have failures, but how they have dealt with those failures. For they are certain to have public failures while in office. If in private life they run from failure or cover it up or rationalize it, are they not likely to do the same in public life? The goal of seeking virtuous people for high office is not to find perfect people, but to find people with the greatest potential to provide, despite their acknowledged limitations (humility being a prudent quality in a leader), the kind of leadership a community needs to flourish. We are not looking for saints to lead us, but we should be looking for people trying to live virtuously and largely succeeding.

It matters little that people will not agree exactly on a list of key virtues. The question of what virtues are most important, and how they should be defined and expressed, should be a fruitful part of an ongoing discussion. But it matters greatly that such a discussion take place. Recent polls indicate a broad recognition that we have a virtue deficit in this country and in its leaders that makes budget deficits pale in importance.

When we are choosing someone to lead us, we do best to look for a "good human being." Such a person is not likely to be moralistic or pious or politically correct. But he or she needs to be virtuous. Because, over time, nations flourish only to the degree that their collective virtue sustains.

CHAPTER 2

WHAT MAKES FOR GOOD LEADERSHIP?

BY ANDY CROUCH

y fellow Americans, the state of our union is strong." So every President over the past several decades has declared in his annual address to Congress. This is a half-truth, even in the best of times. Because a new President will be inaugurated in January 2017, there will likely be no formal State of the Union speech next year. Just as well, because it is hard to imagine anyone saying with a straight face that our union is strong.

This is not the first time America has faced daunting internal tensions and external threats. But during this year's presidential primaries, fear, despair, and dissatisfaction have drawn Americans to would-be leaders who promise radical change to restore our country's strength.

Yet strength is only one part of real health for nations. All truly flourishing communities must also embrace vulnerability. They accept and even seek out meaningful risk for the sake of growth. Great leaders do not just promise strength: They call people to risk as well.

But around the world today we see the rise of leaders who offer various forms of authority without vulnerability—strength without risk. This is the promise of every authoritarian government and every dictator, and it is increasingly the currency of American political campaigns. One candidate promised to build a wall to keep out illegal immigrants from Mexico—and to make Mexico pay for it. Another promised free tuition at public universities—and to make "Wall Street" pay for it.

These promises have several things in common, and not just that they are entirely unfeasible. They promise goods without a price, protection without effort, and benefits without costs—at least to people like us. They depend on extracting the effort and cost from others—others who are treated not as potential partners but as permanent enemies.

We also see a level of bluster in American politics unparalleled since the Jacksonian excesses of the 19th century—proclaiming one's own power and reveling in others' weakness. The unrealistic promises have been matched by crude displays of bravado and disdain for "losers." The same people who flaunt their power complain incessantly, airing their grievances against the powerful forces arrayed against them. Authoritarian leaders flaunt their power, manipulative leaders flaunt their supposed vulnerability—and the most toxic leaders do both at the same time.

Christians, of all people, should be able to resist the temptation to cheer at shallow policy proposals and for politicians who are shallower still. We must recover the politically radical dimensions of the claim that "Jesus is Lord." To say Jesus is Lord is to establish a standard against which all human exercises in power can be judged—and, in time, will be judged.

Jesus never flaunted his power. His public miracles were often followed by deliberate withdrawals from sight—as when the crowds, amazed by the miraculous provision of food, sought to make him king. He chose a title, "Son of Man," that for all its messianic overtones identified him with simple humanity, not godlike invulnerability. He knew that a fatal confrontation was inevitable, but he never stirred up grievances or indulged in self-pity.

No leader, whether religious or political, will always live up to Jesus' standard of leadership. But for this very reason, we need leaders who avoid stoking the worst in us.

America has sometimes had such leaders. John F. Kennedy called the country to "bear the burden of a long twilight struggle, year in and year out, 'rejoicing in hope, patient in tribulation.'" Abraham Lincoln, perhaps the greatest American President, refused to demonize his opponents even as he prosecuted a dreadful war, "with malice toward none, with charity for all, with firmness in the right as God gives us to see the right."

Our real vulnerability is not the result of some easily specified—and eliminated—group of enemies. It is the result of living in a world that would be complex and risky even if it were not also ridden with brokenness and evil. Great leaders resist the temptation to create scapegoats even in the face of difficult choices.

Until Christians ask for that kind of honesty and courage from our leaders, we are likely to continue to prop up the worst kind of American idols.

CHAPTER 3

THE DIFFERENCE FAITH MAKES IN THE WHITE HOUSE

AN INTERVIEW WITH GARY SCOTT SMITH

 o have so many candidates in the current presidential campaign say faith is a significant part of their lives and has a major impact on how they think about politics and policies—this is unique." So says Gary Scott Smith, professor of history at Grove City College in Pennsylvania. He should know. His recent book is titled *Religion in the Oval Office: The Religious Lives of American Presidents* (Oxford University Press).

In this interview with the editors of *Christianity Today,* he discusses what difference, in fact, faith has made in the White House.

In a country that celebrates the separation of church and state, the House of Representatives recently and overwhelmingly reapproved "In God We Trust" as the U.S. motto. This suggests that religion continues to play a significant role in our public life. What is that role?

The role is great. We have a more strident group of agnostics and atheists and non-churched people in our country than we've ever had. We can go back to the group that now calls itself Americans United for the Separation of Church and State (originally called Protestants and Other Americans United for the Separation of Church and State), which started in 1947. Over the past sixty years, this group has complained that we're not properly recognizing the boundaries of the First Amendment. But the issue has become more important in the last ten to fifteen years. So there is more pressure than ever on politicians to be careful about the way they express their faith. We also have so much more media scrutiny than ever.

Some groups say the First Amendment requires that you check your religious values at the door and not bring them into the public square. Polls show that the vast majority of Americans see that as violating the meaning of the First Amendment, especially if we look at what the founders themselves did in the realm of politics. They declared national days of prayer and fasting. They allowed chaplains for the Senate and the House. They allowed military chaplains. The most outspoken separationist, Thomas Jefferson, who gave us the famous statement about the wall of separation between church and state, was okay with the federal government funding evangelistic missions to Native Americans and with allowing worship to take place in the Hall of the House of Representatives when very few congregations were functioning yet in Washington.

Today, the vast majority of Americans agree that the First Amendment says we can't establish a national church, and we can't forbid freedom of worship. But on the other hand, a Christian has the same right to bring his worldview into political discourse as does an atheist or a secular humanist or a Muslim.

What has been the President's religious role in our nation's history?

In the absence of a national chaplain, the President sometimes has functioned in that role partly because of the expectations of the American people. When we have a crisis, whether it is a war or a tragedy—like the shootings in Tucson or a space disaster—we expect the President to function almost as our civic priest. We want him to give us spiritual assurance that God's still in control and that the people who have died have died for a good cause and that they're going to be eternally blessed. President Obama did this in his tenth year anniversary speech for the victims of 9/11 and in the speech he gave in Tucson for the victims of the shooting there. Nearly every President has at some point given speeches where he has acted as a national chaplain, a high priest of civil religion. Of course, they're very careful in those discourses to talk only about God, not Jesus, and to use very generic religious language.

The other potential religious role is for the President to serve as a prophet of civil religion. Abraham Lincoln probably is the greatest example. He tried to stand above the conflict of the Civil War and say that both sides were at fault, both sides needed to repent, both sides needed to be charitable toward one another.

All kinds of polling data show Americans want their chief executive to have strong religious faith. It's usually in the 70 to 75 percent range, depending on how the question is asked. They want to know that their President prays, seeks God's guidance, and believes God's in control of the universe. They typically don't want the President to wear his religion on his sleeve, to be too overtly religious. That scares people; Americans consider that potentially divisive. But they do want their President to be a person of faith.

Some Christians say that civil religion is an alternate, idolatrous faith, one that competes for the Christian's loyalty. Others think it relatively harmless, and others believe it is a positive good—at least up to a point. Where do you stand on that spectrum?

We have a society that is pluralistic. It's diverse. The New Testament doesn't say that we're supposed to use government to impose our values upon other people; everybody should have the same civic rights to propagate their religious convictions. Of course, you don't allow human sacrifice. You don't allow things that are beyond the pale of civic respectability. But Muslims, Buddhists, Hindus, secular humanists, Christians, Jews—everybody should have the same civil rights in society.

So what do you do if you're a Christian President? How do you function? Christian Presidents rightly recognize that they are the President of all the people. How do they effectively follow Christ in the political realm? Well, you probably can't speak explicitly about Jesus, because that would be politically divisive (unless you're talking to Christian groups or making proclamations about specific Christian holidays). So you probably are going to use generic language.

You can debate exactly what civil religion means, and it can be idolatrous. However, I don't think it has to be idolatrous. It would be difficult to pinpoint a time in American history where it's been clearly idolatrous. In a pluralistic society, religious freedom is most consistent with what the New Testament teaches in terms of the role of magistrates; they are not instructed to use their power to force people to believe any particular thing.

Many people believe that most candidate attestations of faith are insincere, just political posturing. What is your impression, especially concerning 20th century Presidents?

You need to look at their entire lives, their faith histories. If you find a consistent pattern, then the idea that they've simply trumpeted their faith to win an election or remain popular loses credibility. You also have to look at what they do and say privately. Ronald Reagan wrote eight or ten handwritten letters a day as President. You can read them to see what he was thinking on a personal level. So you try to look at what people were saying off the record when they didn't expect that anyone else was going to be reading what they wrote.

Obviously, politicians try to present themselves favorably and use everything possible to their advantage. Are they above using faith and religion to do that? Absolutely not. But you have to look at their record of involvement with a church, who they look to as advisers, what they read, and what they say about theological matters. If you take all that into account, and if what they're saying publicly seems consistent with those things that have been an integral part of their lives, then it makes sense to say that it's not just a political ploy. It's a genuine part of their lives.

Among the Presidents you've studied, who have been the most personally devout and theologically orthodox?

In terms of traditional orthodoxy, Woodrow Wilson, Jimmy Carter, and George W. Bush would be at the very top. William McKinley would also be on that list; he was a very devout Methodist.

My book tries to draw correlations and connections between Presidents and public policy. I examined how their faith may have affected their policies while they were in office. Harry Truman was a rather devout man, and he knew the Bible very well and quoted it extensively. Reagan was also close to the top, as was Eisenhower.

If we are simply looking at Presidents who had a strong interest in religion, I'd emphasize John Quincy Adams. I'd also put Thomas Jefferson on that list, because Jefferson extensively studied religious writings and especially the Bible, and he read the Bible probably half an hour a day. And he often read it in French and Italian to get insights that he couldn't glean from English translations.

Which presidential administrations have been most shaped by the chief executive's religious convictions?

Carter's and Wilson's. I would say Truman, too. One place you can clearly see it is in Truman's recognition of Israel. One of the main reasons he went against the entire State Department and George Marshall, his Secretary of State—who were arguing that strategically it wasn't a good move to recognize Israel—was his understanding of the Bible and his belief that the Jews deserved to have a Promised Land. Truman saw himself as a kind of Cyrus giving back the land to the Jews—he said so on the record a couple of times. His administration was shaped substantially by his own personal faith.

Reagan's faith played a substantial role in his presidency. George W. Bush's faith informed his faith-based initiatives and his reasoning regarding his war against terrorists.

I covered eleven Presidents in the first book. I'm doing eleven more in the second book. In all twenty-two cases, you can find correlations between faith and policy. I never argue that a President's faith directly caused him to adopt a certain policy, but I do argue that it's reasonable to conclude that his faith was a strong part of the mix that led him to do what he did.

Are there Presidents whose faith seemed sincere but had no effect on their policies?

I can't think of a single example of that. I might argue that there are Presidents for whom faith was not particularly important and therefore did not have much impact. The leading example would be John F. Kennedy. I included him in my first book because the election of 1960 was pivotal because it brought a Catholic into office. So much of that election pertained to concerns about Kennedy's Catholicism. But as his wife famously said, "I don't know why they were so concerned about his religion. He never was."

How much should citizens, especially Christians, take a candidate's personal faith into account when determining their vote?

I wouldn't make it the number one consideration. The main thing we should look at is the character of the candidate, which is, of course, often connected to his worldview and faith commitments. We should look as much as possible at character issues.

Second, we should look at the whole gamut of policies a candidate promotes and see how that lines up with what we think is best for our nation and most in accordance with our understanding of Scripture. It's certainly possible that a candidate who has weaker faith commitments might advocate policy prescriptions that we would deem to be more in line with what the Scriptures teach.

If everything else were equal, I would be more inclined to support the candidate who has a strong faith and who looks to God for guidance and who covets the prayers of the American people, who is a person of prayer and who's part of a worshipping Christian community. But I would put character and policy analysis first.

In your study of the Presidents and their faith, what has impressed you most?

When you read what these Presidents have said, when you look at their life stories, you find that faith written all over their lives. And yet the modern academic community has largely ignored this. You can read massive tomes about individual Presidents without even catching a glimpse of the fact that they had a deep faith, that their faith meant anything to them. If faith is discussed, it's often portrayed negatively. In the past decade, there's been a growing awareness of the faith of Presidents, but it is instructive to see how much these Presidents wrote about their own faith, how much their faith meant to them, and the connections between their faith and policies.

PART TWO

ELECTION 2016

CHAPTER 4

WHY POLLSTERS MISUNDERSTAND 'THE EVANGELICAL VOTE'

BY ED STETZER & LEITH ANDERSON

T hese days, everyone wants to know what evangelicals believe—especially about political issues.

Researchers have asked evangelicals what they think about same-sex marriage, science, the death penalty, immigration, and, especially, whom they plan to vote for in the upcoming election.

That's understandable. Americans who identify as white evangelicals remain a powerful voting bloc in the United States—representing 1 out of every 5 voters in recent presidential elections, according to The Pew Research Center. And most—about 8 in 10—have voted Republican in at least one election. So it's no surprise that Donald Trump recently proclaimed, "I am an evangelical."

But who is an evangelical? Many pollsters and journalists assume that evangelicals are white, suburban, American, Southern, and

Republican, when millions of self-identifying evangelicals fit none of these descriptions.

One of us (Leith) has led the National Association of Evangelicals (NAE) for a decade. The other (Ed) has led LifeWay Research, one of the largest Christian research groups in the world. We think there is a more coherent and consistent way to understand who evangelicals are—one based on what evangelicals *believe*.

WHY IT MATTERS

The desire to survey white evangelicals to determine their political interests inadvertently ends up conveying two ideas that are not true: that "evangelical" means "white" and that evangelicals are primarily defined by their politics.

But voting isn't the only thing—or the main thing—that most evangelicals do. Politics are important, but politics aren't our defining characteristic, nor should they be.

And clearly not all evangelicals fit the white evangelical category. Our country has become more diverse over the past half-century, and so have evangelical churches. To equate "evangelical" with "white evangelical" leaves out many people with evangelical beliefs.

"You never hear about black evangelicals," Anthea Butler, associate professor of religion at the University of Pennsylvania, said last year. "Watch the 2016 election. When they talk about evangelicals again, they won't go to Bible-believing black evangelicals. They're going to talk to white people."

Surveys that focus on white evangelicals shape the way our non-evangelical neighbors see evangelical believers. So they often perceive us primarily as political adversaries or allies, rather than people primarily motivated by beliefs.

As one unsympathetic political activist put it recently to Leith (without knowing he was president of the NAE), "All those evangelicals really scare me."

But our new definition shows that when we examine them by what they actually believe, American evangelicals are quite diverse.

Researchers look at three factors when studying religious groups. Known as the three *B*s, they are belief, behavior, and belonging. In order to understand any religious group, you have to consider all three.

Yet most public polling on evangelicals has focused only on belonging, asking people to identify with a specific faith tradition. In some cases, people are asked to identify themselves in basic categories like Catholic, Protestant, Jew, Muslim, and so on. Other polls ask people to use labels like "evangelical," "born again," or "fundamentalist." (Pew, for example, combines "evangelical" and "born again.")

More in-depth studies ask respondents the name of their denomination. Researchers then place those responses in a category using a standard set of historical traditions known as RELTRAD (short for religious traditions). For example, if you pick Episcopalian, you are mainline Protestant; if you pick Assemblies of God, you are evangelical.

Those traditions reflect most of the largest faith groups in the United States: evangelicals, mainline Protestants, black Protestants, Jews, and increasingly, Nones—those who claim no religious identity.

Yet asking for religious self-identification isn't enough. For example, many Christians hold evangelical beliefs but don't call themselves evangelical; many Christians call themselves evangelical yet don't hold evangelical beliefs. And denominational ties don't always predict what someone actually believes. There are evangelical Episcopalians, for example, and Pentecostals who are more mainline in their theology.

Race and history are also important factors. A recent LifeWay study of evangelical beliefs found that only 1 in 4 African Americans *who have evangelical beliefs* self-identify as evangelical. That number jumps to about 6 in 10 for whites who hold evangelical beliefs and about 8 in 10 for Hispanic Americans who hold evangelical beliefs.

This study reveals a gap between belief and belonging. As a result, when pollsters refer to "evangelicals," it usually represents a smaller, self-identified subset based on criteria that fail to take into account evangelical beliefs.

But if many individuals don't use the label "evangelical" to describe themselves, is it fair to label them as such if their beliefs correspond with others who do use the evangelical label? Yes, for research purposes—to understand a group of Americans who hold something in common. For example, researchers typically do not rely on people to label themselves as young adults or older adults. The reason is that each respondent will have a different definition in mind. So researchers ask people their age and place them in a category.

BEYOND BEBBINGTON

Over the past few years, a group of evangelical leaders and researchers have worked on addressing the gap between belief and belonging. To do so, we developed a new research-driven definition of evangelical. The refined definition focuses on belief—rather than self-identification or belonging—and should help researchers understand evangelicals better.

Let's start with some basics.

The word *evangelical* comes from the Greek New Testament word *euangelion*; *eu* means "good" and *angelion* means "message." Since *evangelical* means "people of good news," all Christians are in some sense evangelical. But the term was eventually used to refer to Protestants in Europe and, later, a subgroup of Protestants in America.

Still, the Western religious movement that has become known as evangelical did not have a founding document or a single recognized founder. Instead, the movement has morphed over time, alongside several concurrent trends.

Evangelicalism is by nature a diverse movement. Though we affirm the historic creeds, there is no evangelical creed. We don't all read the same books or sing the same songs. Neither do evangelicals agree on how to practice our faith; we disagree over who can preach, how to practice baptism and Communion, or whether we should drink alcohol.

Still, despite all the variety, our research suggests a common set of core beliefs. With early assistance from Ron Sellers, the mind behind Grey Matter Research, we began a two-year process of defining those beliefs through conference calls, meetings, and email exchanges.

At first the broad range of options started looking more like a sermon series than an elevator speech, a book rather than a business card. So we crafted a research definition rather than a theological creed, list of behaviors, or probe of church membership.

This new definition was influenced by the famed Bebbington Quadrilateral, developed by David Bebbington of the University of Stirling in Scotland. Bebbington argued that evangelicals in 18th-century to early 20th-century England had four defining characteristics: biblicism, a love of God's Word; crucicentrism, a focus on Christ's atoning work on the cross; conversionism, the need for new life in Christ; and activism, the need to live out faith in action.

This has become a standard way to understand classic evangelical theological commitments in England and the United States.

These four characteristics were not meant to tell evangelicals what they ought to believe and how they should act. Instead, as Bebbington pointed out in a 2003 interview, they describe what evangelicals have believed and how they have acted.

"I'm a mere historian," Bebbington says. "I simply look at evidence, conceptualize it, and write it up."

Of course, some who identify as evangelical want to broaden, change, or repudiate one or more of these commitments—they want to change the understanding of what an evangelical is. But the changes being offered have yet to win a large consensus. Until they do, we thought it best to stick with a classic set of beliefs that have represented evangelicals for some time.

A group of leaders that included Richard Mouw of Fuller Theological Seminary, Paul Nyquist of Moody Bible Institute, and Mark Noll of the University of Notre Dame helped us turn those four characteristics into a list of 17 questions.

To ensure the questions asked would be helpful to future researchers, we field tested the questions, with the help of LifeWay and with input on the process from sociologists Rodney Stark at Baylor University, Christian Smith at the University of Notre Dame, Penny Marler of Samford University, Nancy Ammerman at Boston University, Mark Chaves at Duke University, Scott Thumma at the Hartford Institute for Religion Research, and Warren Bird of Leadership Network.

Our research suggests that, when it comes to statistical prediction, four belief statements in particular proved extremely helpful. We asked a representative sample of Americans whether they agree or disagree with the following statements:

- The Bible is the highest authority for what I believe.

- It is very important for me personally to encourage non-Christians to trust Jesus Christ as their Savior.

- Jesus Christ's death on the cross is the only sacrifice that could remove the penalty of my sin.

- Only those who trust in Jesus Christ alone as their

Savior receive God's free gift of eternal salvation.

Those who agreed with all four statements were also likely to *self-identify* as evangelicals, thus bridging the gap between belief and belonging. They also attend church on a regular basis—meaning these four questions about belief also correlate with behavior (church attendance).

Though there are many other factors or belief statements many evangelicals would include here, these four, taken together, create a tool that predicts all the other things evangelicals could include.

Do these four questions bring some Christians into evangelicalism who might never call themselves evangelicals? Conversely, are there self-described evangelicals who will be excluded because they don't strongly agree with every one? Yes and yes. That's the case with every research tool.

Even so, the questions help us reliably identify which Americans hold classic evangelical beliefs.

Some evangelicals equate *evangelical* with "real Christian" or "orthodox Christian." The tool does not determine the depth or sincerity of faith—only God can do that. It helps only to clarify which Americans hold these classic evangelical theological commitments.

When all is said and done, about 30 percent of all Americans have evangelical beliefs as described by the four questions. Broken out by ethnicity, 29 percent of whites, 44 percent of African Americans, 30 percent of Hispanics, and 17 percent of people from other ethnicities have evangelical beliefs.

But won't adding one more definition only add to the confusion about the *e* word?

Not as long as we contextualize our definition. We can't say, without qualification, that someone is an evangelical. We need to distinguish between a self-identified evangelical, a person affiliating with an evangelical denomination, or someone with classic evangelical beliefs. These describe evangelicals in different ways, and for the purpose of analysis, they create different subgroups of people.

But we trust that our definition will become a useful tool for researchers to more fully understand who evangelicals are. More important, we hope that as this tool is used, more Americans will see through the unfortunate cultural and political stereotypes and recognize evangelicals as a diverse people of faith who have given their lives to Jesus Christ as their Savior.

CHAPTER 5

THIS ELECTION ISN'T ABOUT ONLY ONE THING

BY MARK GALLI

hree devout Christians made statements early in the primaries that point to the challenge for evangelicals as we step into the muddy waters of another electoral season.

The first comes from Pope Francis. Responding to Donald Trump's views on illegal immigration from our southern border, he said that anyone who wants to build a wall is not "Christian."

I didn't think the Pope was judging Trump's relationship to God (he's said on other occasions, "Who am I to judge?"). I think he was making a moral pronouncement about "the wall": He was saying it would be unchristian—or immoral—to build such a wall.

I trust we never get to a point where morality and policy are completely divorced. But in this instance, as in so many, it's difficult to determine what in fact is the "Christian" position. Despite the ugly rhetoric, Trump and friends are deeply concerned about the security of U.S. citizens. This is a moral concern, a Christian concern—we want to protect

47

the lives and jobs of our fellow citizens. I don't happen to think building a wall is the best way to achieve security, nor the best way to live up to our national ideas of welcoming the "tired," "poor," and "huddled masses yearning to breathe free." My Christian faith informs my judgment. But it would be self-righteous to say that mine is "the Christian position" and that any other is not "Christian."

Many political solutions are rife with moral ambiguity. The security barrier that separates Israel from the West Bank is a deeply troubling phenomenon: it divides people, brings unnecessary hardship to those who must cross it daily to work, and symbolizes the failure of democratic values. But since it has been erected it has saved thousands of lives by thwarting terrorist attacks in Israel. Is the security barrier "Christian"? Is it "moral"? Yes and no.

The second statement came from Jerry Falwell Jr., who recently endorsed Donald Trump. In explaining his endorsement, he said,

> I do not believe, however, that when Jesus said "render unto Caesar the things that are Caesar's" that he meant we should elect only someone who would make a good Sunday School teacher or pastor. When we step into our role as citizens, we need to elect the most experienced and capable leaders.

He's right about this, of course. An apocryphal quote of Martin Luther says, "I'd rather be ruled by a competent Turk than an incompetent Christian." On the other hand, the personal morality of our leaders does affect their leadership. Bill Clinton's sexual exploits while in office distracted his administration, preventing his team from accomplishing anything of significance for months. I don't know that his administration ever quite recovered from his immoral behavior.

In the third and final statement, there's the temptation to judge a candidate by relying on a personal impression. Pastor Mark Burns, a Christian television entrepreneur based in South Carolina, has endorsed Trump. Before meeting Trump, he was "full of apprehension," but he said that he "really wanted to hear the man's heart." Burns explains:

> For those of us who are evangelical leaders and pastors,
> we are led by listening to the spirit of an individual, and
> we also believe that through the Holy Spirit, [it] will
> reveal to us whether someone is truthful or not. All of
> us, especially after that first meeting, and especially us
> in the African American evangelical community, [we]
> came out believing that this person is legit.

We want to support leaders we can trust, and meeting a leader face-to-face often encourages trust. But we evangelicals can be just as gullible as was Neville Chamberlain, who, after meeting with Adolf Hitler in 1939, wrote in his diary that Hitler was a man one could "do business with." I'm not comparing Trump to Hitler, but I am saying that charismatic figures can fool us into trusting them when they are, in fact, not trustworthy in the least.

We are wiser politically to not take a politician's word or read his "heart," no matter how sincere he or she seems. In the end, politics is about effective action, which comes about through specific policies. We should place our trust not so much in leaders who seem trustworthy as those whose actions prove they are.

Listening to another's "heart" blinds us not only to policy but also to morality. This is most evident in Falwell's assessment of Trump:

> I do believe Trump is a good father, is generous to those
> in need, and is an ethical and honest businessman. I have
> gotten to know him well over the last few years and have
> come to admire him for those traits.

It's hard to imagine how Falwell can blithely ignore Trump's founding of gambling casinos and his bragging about the famous women he has slept with—not to mention his habitual arrogance, the very opposite of the Christian virtue of humility. Whatever attractiveness he might have for some, the plain fact is that Trump is not a paragon of virtue.

49

Politics is partly about morality and partly about effectiveness. It's partly about the character of leaders and partly about their ability to lead. That's what makes politics so aggravating, unpredictable, and just plain fascinating. Wisdom is not isolating one aspect, whether that be moral or pragmatic, and using it as the sole criteria, but holding many things in tension. It also means we cast our ballots while praying, "Lord, have mercy."

CHAPTER 6

SHOULD CHRISTIANS VOTE FOR THE LESSER OF TWO EVILS?

BY RUSSELL MOORE

 or years, I have urged Christians to take seriously their obligations as citizens, starting with exercising the right to vote. In the public square and at the ballot box, we must be more engaged, not less.

But what happens in a race where Christians are faced with two morally problematic choices? Should voters cast a ballot for the lesser of two evils? This unpredictable election cycle could go in any number of directions, and I keep getting asked this question.

For starters, unless Jesus of Nazareth is on the ballot, any election forces us to choose the lesser of evils. Across every party and platform, all have sinned and fall short of the glory of God. Still, the question is a valid one. Believing in human depravity doesn't negate our sense of responsibility. By the standard of God's law, every person is a liar, but that doesn't mean we should hire an employee we know has a pattern of lying. Jesus taught that all who have lust in their hearts are adulterers, but that doesn't mean a woman should shrug her shoulders when she learns her potential new husband is a serial philanderer.

When considering the question of choosing between the lesser of two evils, we must begin with what voting is within our system of government. In our system, *citizen* is an office; we too bear responsibility for the actions of the government. Just as the lordship of Christ made demands for public justice on office-holders in the New Testament (Luke 4:15), the same is true for those who rule as citizens.

The apostle Paul taught that the sword of Caesar is given by God to commend good and punish evil (Rom. 13:1-5). The Bible addresses the limits of this role, recounting those who use the sword in unjust ways and are held accountable to judgment (i.e., Rev. 13).

In a democratic republic, the authority over statecraft rests with the people themselves. In the voting booth, we delegate others to swing the sword of public justice on our behalf. If we think of a campaign like a job interview, we cannot ethically contract someone to do evil on our behalf.

Can a candidate make promises about issues then do something different in office? Yes. Can a candidate present a sense of good character in public then later be revealed to be a fraud? Sure. The same happens with pastors, spouses, employees, and in virtually every other relationship. But that sense of surprise and disappointment is not the same as knowingly delegating our authority to someone with poor character or wicked public stances. Doing so makes us as voters culpable. Saying, "the alternative would be worse" is no valid excuse.

Think of military service, another office of public responsibility, as an example. Members of the military don't need to approve of everything a general decides to be faithful to their duty to the country. But if they're commanded to either slaughter innocent non-combatants or desert and sign up with the enemies of one's country, a Christian can't merely choose the least bad of these options. He would have to conclude that both are wrong and he could not be implicated in either. If a Christian doctor were forced to choose between performing abortions or assisting suicides, she could not choose the lesser of these two evils but must conscientiously object.

That said, all political issues are not equal. I've voted for candidates I disagreed with on issues like immigration reform or family medical leave because I've agreed with them on the sanctity of human life. I could not, though, vote for a "pro-life" candidate who is also for racial injustice or war crimes or any number of other first-level moral issues. There are some candidates I agree with on issues like economic growth or national security for whom I could not vote for because they deny the personhood of the unborn or restrict religious freedom for all people.

Given these moral convictions, there have been times when I've faced two candidates, both of whom were morally disqualified. In one case, one candidate was pro-life but a race-baiter, running against a candidate who was pro-choice. I could not in good conscience put my name on either candidate. I wrote in the name of another leader. Other times, I've voted for a minor party candidate.

Candidates from outside the two major parties sometimes win. Abraham Lincoln ran as a Republican in an era when the major parties were the Whigs and Democrats. Even when third-party candidates don't win the election, they can introduce issues and build a movement for the future. Write-in candidates have occasionally won; U.S. Senator Lisa Murkowski of Alaska won her re-election as a write-in candidate in 2010.

In the cases when I've voted for an independent or written in a candidate, I didn't necessarily expect that candidate to win—my main objective was to participate in the process without endorsing moral evil. As Christians, we are not responsible for the reality of our two-party system or for the way others exercise their citizenship, but we will give an account for how we delegate our authority. Our primary concern is not the election night victory party, but the judgment seat of Christ.

When Christians face two clearly immoral options, we cannot rationalize a vote for immorality or injustice just because we deem the alternative to be worse. The Bible tells us we will be held accountable not only for the evil deeds we do but also when we "give approval to those who practice them" (Rom. 1:32).

This side of the New Jerusalem, we will never have a perfect candidate. But we cannot vote for evil, even if it's our only option.

CHAPTER 7

THE HISPANIC QUANDARY: *¿CUÁNDO?*

BY CARLOS CAMPO

In June I joined many evangelicals—a number of Hispanics among them—in New York City for "A Conversation About America's Future with Donald Trump and Ben Carson." Trump was asked a "softball" question by a Hispanic leader: "You have often spoken of building a wall for our southern border, but how will you build a bridge to Hispanics, the fastest growing demographic in our nation?" Trump's answer was hardly satisfactory (more of that to follow). But it isn't as if we Hispanics have a great deal of confidence in Hillary Clinton on this matter. She—and President Obama—voted for the Secure Fence Act in 2006, which would have added 700 miles of double fencing to the border.

As the 2016 Republican and Democratic conventions are now concluded, the pop song titled "Cuándo, Cuándo, Cuándo (When, When, When)" seems to capture Hispanic sentiment about the presumptive candidates in America. While what follows is perhaps presumptive to a fault, it may offer some thoughts from a Hispanic point of view about the "contest of negatives" that is Election 2016. If white Americans are feeling tepid about the final two candidates, Hispanics are perhaps even more disenchanted, wondering when either Trump or Clinton will emerge as a leader Hispanics can entirely support.

CLINTON'S RHETORIC—AND REALITY

Hispanic Democrats—some 60 percent of registered Hispanic voters—are asking when their candidate will respond more fully to this 55 million person and growing minority. To begin with, when will the party's leaders follow through on their lingering promise to reform our broken immigration system? Though we often hear that immigration ranks fourth among issues (after the economy, education, and health care) for Hispanic voters, it is clearly the "gateway issue" for many Hispanics, who are calling on Clinton to deliver what Obama did not. Clinton is saying all the right things. She will create "the first ever Office of Immigrant Affairs." She is "committed to introducing comprehensive immigration reform and a path to legitimate citizenship within the first 100 days of [her] presidency." She will "end family detention, close private immigrant detention centers, and help more eligible people become naturalized." Instead of advocating for building a wall, she promises to "tear down barriers" that have kept Hispanics from succeeding more fully.

Yet as I already noted, many Hispanics like me struggle with the perceived divide between Clinton's rhetoric and her record. In addition to voting for the Secure Fence Act as recently as last year, she seemed to flaunt the fact that she voted "numerous times" for a "barrier" to block illegal immigrants coming from the south. Also, when the Central American immigrant crisis first hit, she was quick to say that deportation was in order. As Latino analyst Alfonso Aguilar notes, "Some Hispanic voters see her as opportunistic."

In addition, some Democratic Catholics and evangelical Hispanics worry that Clinton's abortion stance has followed party lines and diverged from her earlier, more moderate position. The Clintons' abortion mantra has been that it should be "safe, legal, and rare," but recently Hillary has dropped the "R-word" when she speaks about the topic. She has also advocated for ending the pro-life Hyde Amendment, first enacted in 1976 and passed in some form ever since, which prevents taxpayer funding of elective abortions through federal programs like Medicaid. Perhaps most troubling was her recent statement at a Women in the World Conference where she suggested that in order to expand worldwide access to abortion, "deep-seated cultural codes, religious beliefs, and structural biases have to be changed."

For some Hispanics, Clinton has also been sullied by her close association with the Obama presidency. Many Latinos resent Obama for deporting 3 million people and dividing hundreds of thousands of families. Many feel Clinton should have spoken up earlier if she was truly opposed to these actions when she served as Secretary of State. Obama's 2008 election promise to reform immigration became hollow by 2012 and is now seen by some as evidence that the vow was nothing more than a vote-mongering ploy by Clinton's party.

I have spoken to a number of Clinton's Hispanic supporters, "Clintonistas," who believe she will crush Trump in November, fueled by a record Hispanic voter turnout. They point to her 2-1 margin with Latinos over Obama in the 2008 primary and the latest party platform, which calls for a path to citizenship "for law-abiding families who are here," the end of immigration raids against children and families, due process for "those fleeing violence in Central America," and to rescind statutory bans on immigrants who modify their status in the country. They also note that Clinton will benefit from the "nostalgia effect" from some Hispanics who fondly remember Bill Clinton's years in the Oval Office as prosperous ones for them. In addition, Hillary has some long-standing ties to Hispanic leaders, going back to the 1970s and her connection to well-respected union leader Franklin Garcia, about whom she wrote in her 2003 memoir. The depth of her support among Hispanics was solidified when the U.S. Hispanic Chamber of Commerce endorsed her (and now-defunct candidate John Kasich) noting: "Clinton has always stood by our community."

TRUMP'S WALL

Perhaps Clinton is buoyed most with Hispanics because her challenger, Donald Trump, has failed so disastrously at connecting with them. Sure that no one could trump (sorry) Mitt Romney's wooden failure with Latinos, we have watched Trump sink to an unimaginable nadir with our community. His string of offenses against Latinos began with his presidential announcement over a year ago, when he mentioned Mexicans in the same phrase as rapists and drug dealers. It continued with a slur against Jeb Bush, saying he "has to like illegals" because he has a Mexican wife. Then came Trump's attack against District Judge Gonzalo Curiel, who Trump called a "Mexican" and "a hater," saying he could not be an objective judge (Curiel was born in Indiana, and his Mexican father arrived in the States before Trump's Scottish-born mother) of a lawsuit involving Trump's real estate business education venture. For the first time in months, Republican leaders were unified—in their condemnation of Trump's "racist" remarks.

Then there's The Wall. It will be massive, impenetrable, 1,954 miles long, paid for by the Mexican government, and "beautiful." From its first mention, Trump's wall has been the protagonist of his discursive narrative; it is one of the "core principles" of his immigration reform plan; it finds its way into nearly every stump speech; and it has become the iconic trope of unity for his followers and growing separation from Hispanics.

Trump's remarks have led many Latinos to coalesce against him, some joining movements like "¡Nunca Trump!" ("Never Trump!") or "Stand Up to Hate," others claiming they would simply rather not vote at all. For example, staunch conservative Rosario Marin, the former U.S. Treasurer under George W. Bush, says that for the first time in more than two decades, she is not campaigning for the Republican presidential nominee. "He's insulted me, the people I love, the community I represent," she says. "He's for everything I've fought against. There is no way I could ask anybody to vote for him."

Returning to that question asked of Trump at the NYC conversation,

Trump immediately, though inexplicably, fastened on the wall, not the bridge, extolling the limitless virtues of the wall and how it will be good for Mexico and America. This gaffe further convinced many Hispanics present that Trump is either unprepared to serve as President (surely he would have developed some standard response for this kind of question) or simply uncaring about the Hispanic community.

Conservative Latinos, like other conservative Americans, are being urged to "consider the alternative," to "reflect upon the upcoming Supreme Court nominations," and support Trump as some kind of lesser of two evils. Yet, many of us are hesitant as we try to picture ourselves in a voting booth, casting our support for a man who has done little to recover the considerable ground he has lost with Hispanics.

Trump is not without Hispanic supporters. There is a "Latinos/Hispanics for Donald Trump" Facebook page with more than 25,000 likes, and some polls reveal he has narrowed the gap with Clinton among Hispanics. There is also a "Hispanic Patriots for Trump" group as well as the National Diversity Coalition for Trump, but this group doesn't include any of the major Hispanic surrogates we saw for Romney, McCain, or Bush. State Rep. Alonzo Baldonado, who represents a district south of Albuquerque, said he would support Trump, and Trump will need more prominent supporters to step forward if he is to reach the 30 percent threshold with Hispanics that many experts say he will need to win in November.

PART OF THE AMERICAN DREAM

Hispanics' hesitancy regarding Clinton and Trump is illustrated by two infamous fast-food related incidents: Clinton's at Chipotle when she launched her campaign, Trump's at the Trump Tower Grill on Cinco de Mayo. For Clinton, she was sunglassed and insular as she grabbed her side of guacamole and left, but tried to use the visit to show she is not the Armani-clad, Wall Street–financed parody some would make of her. But Hispanics are relational and have heard that the former first lady can often be dismissive of staff. The fact that she did not stop to speak to a single patron or worker is not lost on the Hispanic electorate who wants to get to know her better but has found her reluctant to reveal her more human qualities, preferring instead to deliver carefully rehearsed platitudes. Trump's tone-deaf Taco Bowl tweet—a photo of himself eating a very Americanized taco bowl with the caption, "I love Hispanics"—testified to his disconnectedness from the Hispanic community. Interestingly, Trump is often praised for his treatment of staff, and he claims many Hispanics to be among them. Yet, Trump too is enigmatic for Hispanics, some of whom like his bold style and anti-establishment air, but are jarred by the lack of humility and sensitivity that he often displays.

Hispanics have seen some heartening gains over the past few years, with a decline in the poverty rate, an increase in annual income, and college attendance rates at a higher percentage than whites. Yet, college graduation rates lag for Hispanics, 70 percent of all Hispanic infants today are born to mothers with a high school degree or less, and Hispanics are over-represented among the poor in America. We need a President who will see us as a rich part of the tapestry that is America.

Former New Mexico governor Bill Richardson's advice to candidates in 2008 rings true today: "They need to start talking to Hispanics," he said, "not like an ethnic minority, but as mainstream Americans who are part of the American Dream." Perhaps there is still time for our remaining candidates to connect with us. If it does not happen soon, we will continue to ask: *¿Cuándo?*

CHAPTER 8

THE SILVER LINING IN THIS PRESIDENTIAL RACE

BY CHRIS HORST

lection season is here, and you've probably already heard loads of grumbling about candidates and our political process.

The primaries are only just starting. But like an echo following the American presidential candidates on the trail, our collective eye rolling and ear plugging has become as reliable as the campaign ads themselves.

The despair is not without merit.

Donald Trump has at times lead national polls despite having made his fortune (though he hasn't even done that) by profiteering off the vulnerable and elderly through his casinos and strip clubs. And, Hillary Clinton demands "religious beliefs and structural biases have to be changed" in order to accommodate her beliefs—all while

61

potentially facing a criminal indictment. No wonder citizens are donning sackcloth and ashes.

Amid the lament, however, thoughtful citizens have opportunities to celebrate what is good about this presidential campaign. This can be taken too far, of course. But we can assume a healthy posture between venerating and vilifying this election season for three reasons.

ELECTION SEASON PROPELS THE ECONOMY

We will spend more money on the 2016 presidential election than we spend on school construction for at-risk children.

I fabricated the statement, but it reflects the kind we constantly hear during election season. We think elections are too expensive, too highly influenced by a few mega-donors, and far less worthy than other places we could invest our money. But an underreported reality of election spending is the churn it has on our economy.

Dollars invested in elections don't evaporate. They are investments in democracy. When we hear about candidates raising hundreds of millions of dollars, our shock comes largely from what we believe is "lost money." *What if we had spent that on education, green energy, or . . . [insert your favorite cause]?*

Election coffers aren't a black hole, though. Ask restaurateurs and hoteliers in Iowa and New Hampshire how they feel about election season. Or bumper sticker and button makers. Or junior staffers and canvassers working with campaigns. Or television stations selling airtime or newspapers selling subscriptions and clicks. Elections are big business. They employ thousands of people directly, fuel the businesses of thousands more indirectly, and create serious economic value, no matter our affection for politics.

Deploying the billions in funds raised for elections are people like my

Iowan friends who own a promotional product company that makes many of the shirts, signs, stickers, and other swag adorning our bodies, lawns, and cars during election season. Elections matter to my friends and to their 47 employees.

ELECTION SEASON REMINDS US OF THE BEAUTY OF DEMOCRACY

In places like Afghanistan, Syria, Iran, Russia, North Korea, Cuba, and Zimbabwe, voters have little to no voice in determining the future of their countries. In many instances, dissent is not only forbidden, but squelched. The global political landscape is often unrelentingly bleak.

For instance, a political catastrophe is currently taking shape in the small capital city of Bujumbura, Burundi. Burundi's president, Pierre Nkurunziza, obtained a great deal of power over his 10 years in office. Facing a term limit, Nkurunziza refused to give it up, running for a third term in defiance of Burundi's constitution. Late last year, Burundians witnessed a failed coup and suffered under a surge in violence, prompting over 100,000 people to flee from their country.

Burundi's story is wrenching, but tragically common. My colleagues at HOPE International are praying for the best and preparing for the worst.

The freedom to vote should not be taken for granted. It is a gift enjoyed only by a small percentage of our planet's residents—past and present. In a country like the United States, our founders quite literally entrusted the power to the people. We can complain about our system's effectiveness—about powerful people wielding too much influence or about the unhealthy marriage between faith and politics. But despite its flaws, our system stands in contrast to countries where all the power is controlled by a handful of self-appointed tyrants.

And it's not all bad news. Often because of the work of Christian missionaries, many developing countries feature thriving democracies.

Nations like Botswana, Ghana, Chile, Uruguay, and the Philippines have proven the merits of democratic rule, even with its shortcomings.

ELECTION SEASON GENERATES MEANINGFUL DISCUSSIONS

Many of us have been instructed to avoid discussing politics and religion in order to remain polite and amicable. Broadly speaking, this is terrible counsel. To be sure, we should avoid becoming petty, coercive, and disingenuous while talking about religion and politics. But to heal our deepest divides, we need more honest conversation, not less, about what matters most.

The issues unfolding on the political stage affect us all. The big ideas we'll see in campaign ads and on debate stages have consequences. They will impact our wallets, communities, and families. The more that sane people discuss and disagree *well*, the better off we all will be.

Let's not succumb to cynicism this election season. Lambasting the democratic process often does little more than make us grumpier. It makes our republic feel less human. So let's not confine ourselves to the sidelines or the heckling section this political season. Rather, let us embrace the season with a more positive outlook. It won't be easy. But that doesn't mean our democracy is not worthy of our best efforts. In a way only she can, Marilynne Robinson wrote artfully about the heart of what election season is all about:

> Democracy, in its essence and genius, is imaginative love for and identification with a community with which, much of the time and in many ways, one may be in profound disagreement.

While many of us will disagree profoundly this election season, let's do so in a loving, Christlike manner, resisting the urge to unleash our inner cynic whenever a friend or family member mentions the campaign strategy or policy proposal of a candidate we find unfavorable.

64

PART THREE

HOPE IN TIMES OF POLITICAL DESPAIR

CHAPTER 9

BONHOEFFER'S ADVICE IN POLITICALLY FEARFUL TIMES

BY RYAN HOSELTON

"Let's say there is a ship on the high sea, having a fierce struggle with the waves. The storm wind is blowing harder by the minute. The boat is small, tossed about like a toy; the sky is dark; the sailors' strength is failing. Then one of them is gripped by...whom? what?...he cannot tell himself. But someone is there in the boat who wasn't there before....Suddenly he can no longer see or hear anything, can no longer row, a wave overwhelms him, and in final desperation he shrieks: Stranger in this boat, who are you? And the other answers, I am Fear....All hope is lost, Fear is in the boat."

On January 15, 1933, in a Berlin church, Dietrich Bonhoeffer delivered this haunting allegory in a sermon titled "Overcoming Fear."

Germany was in the midst of fearful and turbulent times, indeed. The devastation of defeat from World War I, just 14 years earlier, was fresh on the people's minds and hearts. The Stock Market Crash of 1929 compounded further pressures on the struggling German economy, driving the number of unemployed to more than six million. The new Weimar

Republic lacked political stability and leadership, and fears of communism and extremism loomed large. As these dark waves battered them from all sides, many Germans—including German Christians—feared what the future would hold.

> "Fear is in the boat, in Germany, in our own lives and in the nave of this church—naked fear of an hour from now, of tomorrow and the day after."

'FEAR HAS CONQUERED US'

Another rising leader took interest in this dire situation, but he offered a quite different solution. Rather than help people overcome their fears, he sought to exploit them for power. With a commanding sense of authority and a persuasive tongue, he offered them a savior: himself.

Just 15 days after Bonhoeffer's sermon, the country made this man, Adolf Hitler, their Chancellor. As Bonhoeffer warned, but could've never foreseen, fear drove Germany—and millions of others—into deeper pain, division, and despair.

> "That is the final triumph of Fear over us, that we are afraid to run away from it, and just let it enslave us. Fear has conquered us."

Many today remember Bonhoeffer for his radical Christian discipleship and sacrificial involvement in the German resistance movement against Hitler. However, few know him for what he believed was most central to his life and ministry: nourishing the body of Christ through the proclamation of the Word. Bonhoeffer cared deeply for the spiritual life and health of the local church, serving in various pastoral roles in Germany, Spain, England, and America. He even wrote his doctoral thesis—*Sanctorum Communio*—on the church as a holy community.

The sermon showcases Bonhoeffer's masterful pastoral instincts. He speaks into this atmosphere of angst and uncertainty with a message of hope—a message the church still needs to hear and re-proclaim today, because no human is beyond fear's reach. We've all encountered its many faces:

> ". . . fear of an important decision; fear of a heavy stroke of fate, losing one's job, an illness; fear of a vice that one can no longer resist, to which one is enslaved; fear of disgrace; fear of another person; fear of dying."

Fear fills us with loneliness, hopelessness, and desperation. It drives us to decisions and actions that undo us.

How does fear do it?

> "It hollows out [our] insides, until [our] resistance and strength are spent and [we] suddenly break down. Fear secretly gnaws and eats away at all the ties that bind a person to God and to others, and when in a time of need that person reaches for those ties and clings to them, they break and the individual sinks back into himself or herself, helpless and despairing."

Fear pollutes our thinking, distorts our judgment, cripples our resilience to evil, dislodges our love, and casts a gloom over our hearts. When fear dominates, then distrust, hatred, and selfishness separate us from our Creator and our neighbor, replacing what unifies us: faith, trust, love.

> "Fear takes away a person's humanity. This is not what the creature made by God looks like."

Millions of Germans allowed fear to erode their humanity, turning from trust in God to trust in a maniac, from love of neighbor to holocaust and war.

Fear has the same power today. We still face the everyday fears that characterize a broken world, in addition to the fears that accompany a tense election year. While the current social and political climate of the United States may not be as extreme as that of Germany in the early 1930s, sensitive church leaders can't help but notice the fear that pervades the current election cycle: a cycle fraught with threats of terrorism, loss of religious freedoms and values, and the risks of immigration. Congregations sense it, fear it, and may even fuel it.

'STRANGELY ENOUGH, ALL OF US ARE AT SEA AGAIN'

Fear doesn't discriminate; it knows no boundaries of time or place.

We often find ourselves in tempestuous waters—yet so did Christ's disciples, Bonhoeffer tells his listeners. He reads Matthew 8:23–27, ending with Jesus' commanding of the storm that terrorized his disciples: "And he said to them, 'Why are you afraid, you of little faith?' Then he got up and rebuked the winds and the sea; and there was a dead calm."

When all hope vanishes, when fear enters the boat, Christ manifests his presence and power over fear.

> "Then it is as if the heavens opened, as if the heavenly hosts themselves raised a shout of victory in the midst of hopelessness: Christ is in the boat. Christ is in the boat, and no sooner has the call gone out and been heard than Fear shrinks back, and the waves subside. The sea becomes calm and the boat rests on its quiet surface. Christ was in the boat!"

The disciples' story is our story, too.

> "We were along on that voyage, weren't we? And the call, 'Christ is in the boat,' was once our salvation too. And now, strangely enough, all of us are at sea again, on that voyage without faith, without hope, overwhelmed, in chains, in bondage, paralyzed by fear; we have lost

heart, lost the joy of living."

Christians are not exempt from storms in life: in fact, fear targets believers more than anyone else.

> "When Christ is in the boat, a storm always comes up. The world tries with all its evil powers to get hold of him, to destroy him along with his disciples; it hates him and rises up against him. Christians surely know this. No one has to go through so much anxiety and fear as do Christians."

This is why, Bonhoeffer insists, we so desperately need the church. The church is where we hear the voice of Christ calling to us, saying, "I am in your boat!" Without it, we'd listen to other voices: voices telling us there is no hope, no way out. Voices telling us to channel our fears for wretched ends. Voices telling us to rest our hope in men, in revolutions, or in ourselves.

> "But look here, right in the middle of this fearful world is a place that is meant for all time, which has a peculiar task that the world doesn't understand. It keeps calling over and over but always anew, in the same tone, the same thing: Fear is overcome; don't be afraid. In the world you are frightened. But be comforted; I have conquered the world! Christ is in the boat! And this place, where this kind of talk is heard and should be heard, is the pulpit of the church. From this pulpit the living Christ himself wants to speak, so that wherever he reaches somebody, that person will feel the fear sinking away, will feel Christ overcoming his or her fear."

The church is a lighthouse in our storm of fears, guiding us away from the rocks with a beaming light pointed at Christ.

When we're overwhelmed with fear, our tendency is to isolate ourselves. But according to Bonhoeffer, "the call of the church" directs us to "suffer and make our way through together with Christ, looking always to him who is with us in the boat."

'YES, THY WILL IS BEING DONE'

When our faith is weak, the church reminds us that it's not the strength of our faith that carries us through our fears, but the strength of our Savior. In moments of despair, when we believe God has left us and no longer cares about the chaos in our lives, the church "takes the cross and places it before our eyes and asks: Did God abandon him? And since God did not abandon Jesus, we will not be abandoned by God, either."

> "The human being doesn't have to be afraid; we should not be afraid! . . . We know that there is hope, and this hope is called: Thy will be done, yes, thy will is being done."

The church reminds us of God's good purposes for our lives, his love for his children, and his power to overcome fear and evil. It tells us truth we don't usually want to hear but so desperately need, offering an alternative to indulging and following our fears.

If there is no storm in our lives at the moment, Bonhoeffer says to hold tight, because dark clouds are always forming. But fear not: God has given us all we need to withstand it.

> "The Bible, the gospel, Christ, the church, the faith— all are one great battle cry against fear in the lives of human beings."

And when fear hits, when we feel alone and helpless, the church will remind us that Christ is in the boat. Then together, we will stand in wonder and declare: "What sort of man is this?"

[All quotes come from Dietrich Bonhoeffer, "Overcoming Fear," in The Collected Sermons of Dietrich Bonhoeffer, *ed. and trans. by Isabel Best (Minneapolis, MN: Fortress Press, 2012), 59–66.]*

CHAPTER 10

GLADLY DOING OUR CIVIC DUTY

BY CHARLES COLSON, WITH ANNE MORSE

 have been surprised by the number of Christians who have given up on politics, especially in the middle of a presidential election. "I don't like any of the candidates, so I'm staying home," some say.

I get fed up with the vain posturing and empty promises, too. But *not* voting is not an option—it's both our civic and sacred duty. Voting is required of us as good citizens and as God's agents for appointing leaders.

How do we go about choosing the best candidates? Not by pulling a partisan lever—that's knee-jerk ideology. Christians live instead by revealed truth, never captive to any party. Thus, the best place to go for wisdom is not the candidates' websites, but the Bible.

Moses' father-in-law, Jethro, advised him to appoint as rulers "able men" who "fear God, men who are trustworthy and who hate a bribe." The standard is competence and integrity. Later, God ordered Samuel to pick Saul, who "shall save my people from the hand of the

Philistines." This passage reminds us of Paul's teaching in Romans: Government's role is to wield the sword to preserve order and restrain evil. So we should seek leaders best able to do that and to pursue justice.

Today, God no longer chooses our leaders directly (although some of us wish he did, if only to spare us the years-long political campaigns). We live in a democracy, so God entrusts to us the job of choosing leaders he will anoint. (Deuteronomy 1:12–13 shows us that democratic principles go directly back to the Old Testament.) Like Samuel, we are commissioned to choose leaders of competence, virtue, and character. That's why not voting or rejecting candidates because they are not perfect on some biblical or political score sheet is a dereliction of our trust.

So is voting for a candidate simply because he is a Christian—startling as this may sound. Rather than checking on the candidates' denomination, we should look for the ablest candidate. Martin Luther famously said he would rather be ruled by a competent Turk—that is, a Muslim—than an incompetent Christian.

In casting a vote, judgment should ultimately be guided by what we perceive to be the common good, a term not often heard in today's special interest-charged political debates. Our founders understood this, which is why they used the term commonweal, or commonwealth. But today's politicians pander to special interests, as we see time and again whenever congressmen dump billions of dollars into earmarks, paying off special pleaders.

But if we look at politics from God's perspective, we see that he has a deep and abiding interest in all people being treated fairly. If God favors any "special interest group," it is the poor, the hungry, the unborn, the handicapped, the prisoner—those with the least access to political power.

This is why we Christians should never allow ourselves to be, as the press has often characterized us, just another special interest group pleading for our agendas only. But if we were a special interest group, we would be lobbying for the dignity of all, especially those who can't always speak for themselves.

So maybe a particular candidate isn't going to cut your taxes or vote for your favorite program, but the real question is, will he serve all the people, or only the loudest?

After considering these criteria, if you are still tempted to stay home on primary or Election Day, dust off your copy of *The City of God*, in which Augustine introduces us to the idea that we live in both the City of God and the City of Man. In describing them, he reiterated Jesus' teaching that while Christians live in the City of Man, they do not belong to it. We are like sojourners in a foreign country; our true home is the City of God.

But Augustine also taught that if we are to enjoy the blessings of the City of Man, we must assume the obligations of citizenship. Instead of doing our civic duty out of compulsion, the Christian does it gladly, out of obedience to God and love of neighbor.

Augustine's teaching also helps us to put the coming election into perspective. Some will be jubilant over the outcome, others bitterly disappointed. But regardless of the returns, the City of God endures. When Augustine was informed that his beloved city of Rome was in flames, his response was that the City of Man is built by man and can be destroyed by man, but the City of God is built by God and cannot be destroyed.

On Election Day we should be the best of citizens, voting for the candidate best for all the people.

And then the next day, after indulging in your celebration—or pity party—get busy working to advance God's kingdom in this earthly society.

A THEOLOGICAL GUIDE TO 7 KEY ISSUES

BY THE NATIONAL ASSOCIATION
OF EVANGELICALS

1. RELIGIOUS FREEDOM AND LIBERTY OF CONSCIENCE

God has ordained the two co-existing institutions of church and state as distinct and independent of each other with each having its own areas of responsibility (Rom. 13:1–7; Mark 12:13–17; Eph. 4:15–16, 5:23–32). We affirm the principles of religious freedom and liberty of conscience, which are both historically and logically at the foundation of the American experiment. They are properly called the First Freedom and are now vested in the First Amendment. The First Amendment's guarantees of freedom of speech, association, and religion provide the political space in which we can carry out our differing responsibilities. Because human beings are responsible to God, these guarantees are crucial to the exercise of their God-given freedom. As God allows the wheat and tares to grow together until the harvest, and as God sends the rain on the just and on the unjust, so those who obey and those who disobey God coexist in society and share in its blessings (Matt. 5:45, 13:24–30). This "gospel pluralism" is foundational to the religious liberty of all.

Participating in the public square does not require people to put aside their beliefs or suspend the practice of their religion. All persons should have equal access to public forums, regardless of the religious content or viewpoint of their speech. Likewise, judicial standards should protect and respect not only religiously compelled practices, but also religiously motivated behavior.

The First Amendment's Establishment Clause is directed only at government and restrains its power. Thus, for example, the clause was never intended to shield individuals from exposure to the religious views of nongovernmental speakers. Exemptions from regulations or tax burdens do not violate the Establishment Clause, for government does not establish religion by leaving it alone. When government assists nongovernmental organizations as part of an evenhanded educational, social service, or health care program, religious organizations receiving such aid do not become "state actors" with constitutional duties. Courts should respect church autonomy in matters relating to doctrine, polity, the application of its governing documents, church discipline, clergy and staff employment practices, and other matters within the province of the church (Acts 18:12–17).

Religion is not just an individual matter, but also refers to rich communal traditions of ultimate belief and practice. We resist the definition of religion becoming either radically individualized or flattened out to mean anything that passes for a serious conviction. Thus, while the First Amendment protects religiously informed conscience, it does not protect all matters of sincere concern.

2. FAMILY LIFE AND THE PROTECTION OF CHILDREN

From Genesis onward, the Bible tells us that the family is central to God's vision for human society. God has revealed himself to us in the language of family, adopting us as his children (Rom. 8:23, Gal. 4:5) and teaching us by the Holy Spirit to call him Abba Father (Rom. 8:15, Gal. 4:6). Marriage, which is a lifetime relationship between one man and one woman, is the predominant biblical icon of God's relationship with his people (Isa. 54:5; Jer. 3:20, 31:32; Ezek. 16:32; Eph. 5:23, 31–32). In turn, family life reveals something to us about God, as human families mirror, however faintly, the inner life of the Trinity.

The mutuality and service of family life contrast strongly with the hypermodern emphasis on individual freedom and rights. Marriage, sexuality, and family life are fundamental to society. Whether we are married or single, it is in the family that we learn mutual responsibility, we learn to live in an ordered society with complementary and distinct roles, we learn to submit and to obey, we learn to love and to trust, we learn both justice and mercy, and we learn to deny ourselves for the well-being of others. Thus the family is at the heart of the organic functioning of society.

Government does not have the primary responsibility for guaranteeing wholesome family life. That is the job of families themselves and of other institutions, especially churches.

But governments should understand that people are more than autonomous individuals; they live in families and many are married. While providing individuals with ways to remedy or escape abusive relationships, governments should promote laws and policies that strengthen the well-being of families.

Many social evils—such as alcohol, drug, gambling, or credit-card abuse; pornography, sexual libertinism, spousal or child sexual abuse; easy divorce, abortion on demand—represent the abandonment of responsibility or the violation of trust by family members, and they seriously impair the ability of family members to function in society. These evils must be viewed not only as matters of individual sin and dysfunction, but also as violations of family integrity. Because the family is so important to society, violations of its integrity threaten public order. Similarly, employment, labor, housing, health care, and educational policies concern not only individuals but seriously affect families. In order to strengthen the family, we must promote biblical moral principles, responsible personal choices, and good public policies on marriage and divorce law, shelter, food, health care, education, and a family wage (James 5:1–6).

Good family life is so important to healthy human functioning that we oppose government efforts to trespass on its territory: whether by encroaching on parental responsibilities to educate their children, by treating other kinds of households as the family's social and legal equivalent, or by creating economic disincentives to marriage. We commit ourselves to work for laws that protect and foster family life, and against government attempts to interfere with the integrity of the family. We also oppose innovations such as same-sex "marriage." We will work for measures that strengthen the economic viability of marriages and families, especially among the poor. We likewise commit ourselves to work within the church and society to strengthen marriages, to reduce the rate of divorce, and to prepare young adults for healthy family life.

3. SANCTITY OF HUMAN LIFE

Because God created human beings in his image, all people share in the divine dignity.

And because the Bible reveals God's calling and care of persons before they are born, the preborn share in this dignity (Ps. 139:13).

We believe that abortion, euthanasia, and unethical human experimentation violate the God-given dignity of human beings. As these practices gain social approval and become legitimized in law, they undermine the legal and cultural protections that our society has provided for vulnerable persons. Human dignity is indivisible. A threat to the aged, to the very young, to the unborn, to those with disabilities, or to those with genetic diseases is a threat to all.

The book of Genesis portrays human attempts to transcend creaturely humility before God as rebellion against God. Christians must witness in the political sphere to the limits of our creatureliness and warn against the dangers of dissatisfaction with human limits.

As many others in the West, we have had such faith in science and its doctrine of progress that we are unprepared for the choices biotechnology now brings us. We urge evangelicals with specialized scientific knowledge to help Christians and policymakers to think through these issues. As technologies related to cloning and creating inheritable genetic modifications are being refined, society is less able to create a consensus on what is good and what limits we should place on human modification. The uniqueness of human nature is at stake.

Where the negative implications of biotechnology are unknown, government ought to err on the side of caution. Christians must welcome and support medical research that uses stem cells from adult donors and other ethical avenues of research. But we must work toward complete bans on human cloning and embryonic stem-cell research, as well as for laws against discrimination based on genetic information.

4. JUSTICE AND COMPASSION FOR THE POOR AND VULNERABLE

Jesus summed up God's law by commanding us to love God with all that we are and to love our neighbors as ourselves (Matt. 22:35–40). By deed and parable, he taught us that anyone in need is our neighbor (Luke 10:29–37). Because all people are created in the image of God, we owe each other help in time of need.

God identifies with the poor (Ps. 146:5–9), and says that those who "are kind to the poor lend to the Lord" (Prov. 19:17), while those who oppress the poor "show contempt for their Maker" (Prov. 14:31). Jesus said that those who do not care for the needy and the imprisoned will depart eternally from the living God (Matt. 25:31–46). The vulnerable may include not only the poor, but also women, children, the aged, persons with disabilities, immigrants, refugees, minorities, the persecuted, and prisoners. God measures societies by how they treat the people at the bottom.

God's prophets call his people to create just and righteous societies (Isa. 10:1–4, 58:3–12; Jer. 5:26–29, 22:13–19; Amos 2:6–7, Amos 4:1–3, 5:10–15). The prophetic teaching insists on both a fair legal system (which does not favor either the rich or the poor) and a fair economic system (which does not tolerate perpetual poverty). Though the Bible does not call for economic equality, it condemns gross disparities in opportunity and outcome that cause suffering and perpetuate poverty, and it calls us to work toward equality of opportunity. God wants every person and family to have access to productive resources so that if they act responsibly they can care for their economic needs and be dignified members of their community. Christians reach out to help others in various ways: through personal charity, effective faith-based ministries, and other nongovernmental associations, and by advocating for effective government programs and structural changes.

Economic justice includes both the mitigation of suffering and also the restoration of wholeness. Wholeness includes full participation in the life of the community. Health care, nutrition, and education are important ingredients in helping people transcend the stigma and agony of poverty and re-enter community. Since healthy family systems are important for nurturing healthy individuals and overcoming poverty, public policy should encourage marriage and sexual abstinence outside marriage, while discouraging early onset of sexual activity, out-of-wedlock births, and easy divorce. Government should also hold fathers and mothers responsible for the maintenance of their families, enforcing where necessary the collection of child-support payments.

Restoring people to wholeness means that governmental social welfare must aim to provide opportunity and restore people to self-sufficiency. While basic standards of support must be put in place to provide for those who cannot care for their families and themselves, incentives and training in marketable skills must be part of any well-rounded program. We urge Christians who work in the political realm to shape wise laws pertaining to the creation of wealth, wages, education, taxation, immigration, health care, and social welfare that will protect those trapped in poverty and empower the poor to improve their circumstances.

We further believe that care for the vulnerable should extend beyond our national borders. American foreign policy and trade policies often have an impact on the poor. We should try to persuade our leaders to change patterns of trade that harm the poor and to make the reduction of global poverty a central concern of American foreign policy. We must support policies that encourage honesty in government, correct unfair socioeconomic structures, generously support effective programs that empower the poor, and foster economic development and prosperity. Christians should also encourage continued government support of international aid agencies, including those that are faith based.

Especially in the developing world, extreme poverty, lack of health care, the spread of HIV/AIDS, inadequate nutrition, unjust and unstable economies, slavery and sexual trafficking, the use of rape as a tool of terror and oppression, civil war, and government cronyism and graft create the conditions in which large populations become vulnerable.

We support Christian agencies and American foreign policy that effectively correct these political problems and promote just, democratic structures.

5. HUMAN RIGHTS

Because God created human beings in his image, we are endowed with rights and responsibilities. In order to carry out these responsibilities, human beings need the freedom to form associations, formulate and express beliefs, and act on conscientiously held commitments.

As recipients of God's gift of embodied life, people need food, nurture, shelter, and care.

In order to fulfill their God-given tasks, all people have a right to private property. God's design for human existence also implies a right to marry, enjoy family life, and raise and educate children. While it is not the primary role of government to provide everything that humans need for their well-being, governments are obligated to ensure that people are not unjustly deprived of them and to strengthen families, schools, businesses, hospitals, social-service organizations, and other institutions so they can contribute to human welfare. At the same time, government must fulfill its responsibilities to provide for the general welfare and promote the common good.

Governments should be constitutionally obligated to protect basic human rights.

Documents like the UN's Universal Declaration of Human Rights are attempts to articulate the kind of treatment that every person deserves from the government under which they live. Insofar as a person has a human right, that person should be able to appeal to an executive, legislative, or judicial authority to enforce or adjudicate that right.

We believe that American foreign policy should reward those countries that respect human rights and should not reward (and prudently employ certain sanctions against) those countries that abuse or deny such rights. We urge the United States to increase its commitments to developing democracy and civil society in former colonial lands, Muslim nations, and countries emerging from Communism.

Because the Creator gave human beings liberty, we believe that religious liberty, including the right to change one's religion, is a foundational right that must be respected by governments (Article 18, Universal Declaration of Human Rights). Freedom of expression and freedom of assembly are closely related to religious liberty, and people must be free to express their vision for a just social order without fear of torture or other reprisal. We also oppose the expansion of "rights talk" to encompass so-called rights such as "same-sex marriage" or "the right to die." Inappropriately expanded rights language has begun to function as a trump card in American discourse that unfairly shuts down needed discussion.

America has a tragic history of mistreating Native Americans, the cruel practice of slavery, and the subsequent segregation and exploitation of the descendants of slaves.

While the United States has achieved legal and social equality in principle, the legacy of racism still makes many African Americans, Hispanics, and other ethnic minorities particularly vulnerable to a variety of social ills. Our churches have a special responsibility to model good race relations (Rom. 10:12). To correct the lingering effects of our racist history, Christians should support well-conceived efforts that foster dignity and responsibility.

6. PEACEMAKING

Jesus and the prophets looked forward to the time when God's reign would bring about just and peaceful societies in which people would enjoy the fruits of their labor without interference from foreign oppressors or unjust rulers. But from the beginning, Christians have recognized that God did not call them to bring in God's kingdom by force. While all Christians have agreed that governments should protect and restore just and peaceful social orders, we have long differed on when governments may use force and whether we may participate in government-authorized force to defend our homelands, rescue others from attack, or liberate other people from oppression.

The peaceful settling of disputes is a gift of common grace. We urge governments to pursue thoroughly nonviolent paths to peace before resorting to military force. We believe that if governments are going to use military force, they must use it in the service of peace and not merely in their national interest. Military force must be guided by the classical just-war principles, which are designed to restrain violence by establishing the right conditions for and right conduct in fighting a war. In an age of nuclear and biological terrorism, such principles are more important than ever.

We urge followers of Jesus to engage in practical peacemaking locally, nationally, and internationally. As followers of Jesus, we should, in our civic capacity, work to reduce conflict by promoting international understanding and engaging in non-violent conflict resolution.

7. GOD'S CREATION

As we embrace our responsibility to care for God's earth, we reaffirm the important truth that we worship only the Creator and not the creation. God gave the care of his earth and its species to our first parents. That responsibility has passed into our hands. We affirm that God-given dominion is a sacred responsibility to steward the earth and not a license to abuse the creation of which we are a part. We are not the owners of creation, but its stewards, summoned by God to "watch over and care for it" (Gen. 2:15). This implies the principle of sustainability: our uses of the Earth must be designed to conserve and renew the Earth rather than to deplete or destroy it.

The Bible teaches us that God is not only redeeming his people, but is also restoring the whole creation (Rom. 8:18–23). Just as we show our love for the Savior by reaching out to the lost, we believe that we show

84

our love for the Creator by caring for his creation.

Because clean air, pure water, and adequate resources are crucial to public health and civic order, government has an obligation to protect its citizens from the effects of environmental degradation. This involves both the urgent need to relieve human suffering caused by bad environmental practice. Because natural systems are extremely complex, human actions can have unexpected side effects. We must therefore approach our stewardship of creation with humility and caution.

Human beings have responsibility for creation in a variety of ways. We urge Christians to shape their personal lives in creation-friendly ways: practicing effective recycling, conserving resources, and experiencing the joy of contact with nature. We urge government to encourage fuel efficiency, reduce pollution, encourage sustainable use of natural resources, and provide for the proper care of wildlife and their natural habitats.

From: *For the Health of the Nation: An Evangelical Call to Civic Responsibility*, copyright © 2004 National Association of Evangelicals. A full copy of this document can be found at *www.nae.net/government-relations/for-the-health-of-the-nation*.

56165682R00049

Made in the USA
Lexington, KY
14 October 2016